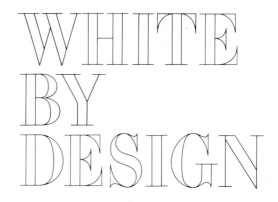

WHITE
BY
DESIGN

WHITE BY DESIGN

BO NILES

Foreword by Ralph Lauren
Principal Photography by Keith Scott Morton
Design by Julio Vega

Stewart, Tabori & Chang
New York

For my family

Editor   Marya Dalrymple
Production coordinator   Nan Jernigan

Text © 1984 by Bo Niles

Originally published in hardcover in 1984

Paperback edition published in 1992 by
Stewart, Tabori & Chang, Inc.
575 Broadway, New York, New York 10012

Library of Congress Cataloging in Publication Data
Niles, Bo.
   White by design.

   White in interior decoration.   I. Title.
NK2115.5.C6N55 1984   747'.94   84-228
ISBN 0-941434-54-0 (cloth)
        1-55670-277-9 (paper)

Distributed in the U.S. by Workman Publishing,
708 Broadway, New York, New York 10003
Distributed in Canada by Canadian Manda Group,
P.O. Box 920 Station U, Toronto, Ontario M8Z 5P9

Text set in Bodoni
Printed and bound in Japan by Toppan Printing Company,
Ltd., Tokyo, Japan

10 9 8 7 6 5 4 3 2 1

*Front cover: Wicker furniture from the collection of Pamela
McGinley Scurry, the Wicker Garden, New York City
Back cover, top: Bedroom in an eastern Long Island beach
house; bottom: Overscaled sofa in a Connecticut barn
re-designed by artist Paul Leonard*

CONTENTS

FOREWORD

White in design has no competition. White in design owns its own world. For expressing purity—whether in a beautiful linen suit, a cotton T-shirt, or a towel—white is simple, elegant, and fresh. It takes a great deal of courage to design in white, and it also takes no courage at all. It is easy and yet it makes a strong statement. White points out the essence of a design concept and expresses every texture, every shape, every mood.

In my own life and in my home, white is everywhere. With all the textures, colors, patterns, and people I work with, I wanted my home to be totally pure, to be a statement that was honest and clean, straight from the heart, a dream. I wanted a place that would give me the feeling of floating. I wanted to come home and feel simplicity and peace.

My apartment enjoys a beautiful view; and white allows everything inside to fade out and the view to come in. I find that white walls are a canvas for anything you put in front of them. There is nothing like an old table, or a painting from any era, placed against a white wall.

There are many whites, and they change with the day, with the sun, and with age. White can be very cool, but it can also be warm and cozy. I mix white with different woods and different accents—white feels different in different places.

No matter what the trend, no matter what the color of the moment is, I always come back to white.

Ralph Lauren

INTRODUCTION

About twenty-five years ago, while working as a
magazine editor and becoming involved with and
interested in the fields of architecture and interior
design, I began to clip and file photographs of
places that I liked and considered well designed.
Reviewing my files some years later, I discovered
that most of the rooms—and houses, too—that had
captivated me initially and still struck me most
forcefully were intentionally designed all in white.
They appeared unaffected by style, yet were some-
how innately, timelessly stylish. In the white
rooms, free of the insistence of chromatic nuance
and innuendo, I saw—and could focus on—the
very essences of space and light, and I found, too,
that shape, texture, and silhouette became inti-
mately revealed in their own purity. In these rooms I
sensed an unequivocal and personal sense of place.

When I talked with the people who inhabited
these rooms and who eventually would inhabit this
book, they spoke first and most intensely of trying
to achieve an individuality, unencumbered by the
constraints of decorating trends. They found they
could best effect this by dissolving a room of color.
The effort in some cases occurred all at once, in one
grand sweep of white; in others, it evolved over

time. But the end result was always a white room, expressive of its owner's unique personality and evocative of a mood or attitude rather than of a decorating style.

But these people spoke also (and unanimously) of oasis, of relief, and of release from the visual cacophony that they felt assaulted them in their everyday lives. In their white rooms, they said, they found refuge from pressure, and a place of absolute and harmonious comfort.

The idea of comfort in design may appear obvious, and it is, of course, primitive and universal as a measure of the human instinct for survival; but in many places where a decorating fad predominates, comfort in shelter and habitat is often ignored or played down.

Architects Kent Bloomer and Charles Moore, considering the vital relationship of the body to its environment, write that perception of design is not merely visual—not merely a recognition of form and structure, and of ornament and decoration—but is an urgent biological response to our surroundings, emanating from the innermost self outward and involving all the senses in a constant longing for balance and harmony. Although we may intuit this longing, we can be distracted from satisfying it by the intervention of other stimuli with our senses. Certainly, a significant element of our visual sense (which is primary among human senses) is its reaction to the stimulus of color.

Color perception is the first triumph of the human intellect. Newborn infants open their eyes to bright white light, but within moments the intensity of the glare is tempered by an awareness of shadow. In time, the infant begins to notice colors.

Scientists have discovered and documented that the eye, as it receives a color, spontaneously and simultaneously "corrects" that hue by counteracting it with its complement in an ongoing effort to

return, for visual comfort, to white. Art theorist Rudolph Arnheim states that "the juxtaposition of complementary colors gives rise to an experience of balance and completeness. The underlying kinship of white [as the luminous fusion of all colors] must be the reason for this. White is undemanding physiologically, for it is the harmony perpetually established in the eye."

White therefore bestows a feeling of equilibrium and calm and evokes a profound subconscious realization of well-being. People who inhabit white rooms not only are liberated from the dictates of decorating fads, but ultimately realize a biological bonus in their own subliminal reaction to the whites they select.

The many designers and architects represented in these pages said that working in white presented the consummate challenge, stretching their imaginations beyond specific stylistic demands toward new visions of space. White rooms became testing grounds for their visions—places where they could refine their art and express it using precise techniques and materials of superb quality.

Many high-quality materials, in their purest, most unadulterated state, are, in fact, white or near-white. Natural fibers, such as cotton, linen, and wool, best display their texture (and the weave in fabrics) in their neutral or bleached form. Many varieties of marble and stone display their grain and weight most clearly and impressively in white. And, while white reveals the integrity of such natural materials, it also elucidates the composition of many man-made materials, such as glazed ceramics, matte or glossy plastics, frosted glass, or even enameled metal.

White, at the last, is more than white. White is chameleon, sensitive to every hue. It absorbs tint and tinge, and thereby persuasively enhances itself. White, conjoined with light, may warm or cool, brighten or soften; it may appear opaque or translucent. White thus becomes infinite in its variety, expressive of many moods.

In this book, therefore, I have grouped the white rooms according to mood: six attitudes in all. Romantic rooms, evocative of times gone by, are gently nostalgic, yet infused with a subtle eroticism that grants them a sparkle and a measure of fantasy.

Country-style rooms, rustic spaces, breathe a freshness and simplicity that is at once ingenuous and wholesome. These rooms appear sturdy, yet richly textured; they are warm, cozy, welcoming.

Rooms I term refined possess a serene confidence born of a heightened sensibility for balance and proportion, which sustains the sense of calm even when the combination of furnishings and accessories at first appears unlikely. A sure sophistication marks these rooms, as well as a polite restraint and dignity in repose.

Rational rooms honor the aesthetic that is purely architectural in concept and scope. Cerebral exercises in the integration of function and form, these rooms reflect precise calculations; their renderings of mathematical precepts lucidly express an intellectual intent.

Introspection and thoughtfulness permeate the atmosphere of rarefied rooms. Sometimes shrouded in mystery, always suggestive of harmonics of mind, these rooms appear elusively resonant, bringing the viewer to a contemplative state and gradually revealing the many levels of thought they accommodate.

Resort rooms offer escape, in the most uninhibited sense. Carefree rooms, they invite impetuous, even hedonistic rejuvenation of mind and body. Enjoy the intensity of pure sensation, they seem to say, and live more fully.

In reflecting emotional states of mind, white rooms bring us to a consciousness of design that is immediate, alive, indelible—and beyond style. White rooms allow us to look at design in its essential state and for its eternal meaning, not for what it could be or should be. Evocative and elemental, white rooms are a tranquil, secure, personal expression of self—at home, in comfort, and at peace.

ROMANTIC WHITES

soothe and caress
in their innocent embrace

Long, long ago, in lands of make-believe and fairy tale, princes and princesses lived happily ever after in castles whose exquisite white turrets extended into cloudless skies. Similarly, in real-life Europe, shimmering white chateaux, such as Chenonceaux and Chambord and Azay-le-Rideau in France and the castles conceived by King Ludwig in Bavaria, were serene and elegant, offering an antidote to the chaotic surrounding world. Recollections of such places inspire a mood of charmed mystery; and their fanciful air is renewed in romantic rooms today.

The gently nostalgic rooms that open this book evoke the mystique of times and places long past. Delving into fantasy, they touch us and enchant us with their tender, dreamlike serenity. Romantic rooms welcome every moment as an occasion for intimacy and delight. In so doing, they suggest a subtle, almost intangible undercurrent of eroticism—but it is an eroticism tinged with the innocence of pure fable. White in these rooms enhances their allure, but it does so in a clear, clean, and unsullied way.

Rarely modern in tone, romantic rooms tend to indulge in souvenirs of the past, enlisting furnishings and accessories reminiscent of other eras. The curvilinear furniture typical of French salons and boudoirs during the time of Louis XV, for example, or the whimsical wicker favored by the Victorians is perfectly suited to today's romantic setting.

When a romantic room does exhibit a more contemporary demeanor, the furnishings ingratiate themselves through a softened silhouette, a graceful scale, a caressing texture. All pieces, whether antique or modern, are arranged to encourage companionship and amity.

The white fabrics found in romantic rooms are supple, often sheer, and may include diaphanous cottons, clinging silks, exotic wools, and crisp yet crushable linens. They may float about a window or tumble down around a table or bed. Sometimes antique linens will add their own ethereal appeal; or treasured laces, gossamer-soft yet resilient, will lend a whisper of delicacy to a bed or loveseat or pillow.

The light that suffuses romantic rooms is hushed, echoing the affectionate glow of dusk or dawn. When the sun seeps directly into a space, it is filtered by lace or lattice to spark playful, teasing patterns across a floor or wall. At night, candlelight may dance and flicker from tapers set in every room.

Romantic rooms are lighthearted in spirit and genial in temperament. They captivate and prevail upon us to linger in their sensitive, soothing embrace.

Although many moods are expressed in this airy house situated near the beach on eastern Long Island, their gentle combination—rustic, resort, refined—conspire to create an endearing and finally very romantic atmosphere. First and foremost, this house fosters a loving concern for friends. It is the clean, warm light that initially welcomes, caressing the free-flowing spaces and playing across floors, walls, and graciously proportioned furnishings. But the small touches embrace even more: Precious antique linens that might have remained tucked away in drawers softly emerge to dapple every bedroom in an inspired gesture of trust and sharing. Along walls, white flowers perpetually bloom. In a guest bedroom, overleaf, the one decorative blossom is actually an enameled cast-iron doorstop.

In the same Long Island house, bedrooms that could have shown a Spartan temperament are instead visually softened by linens and refreshed by an eclectic mix of furnishings and accessories united in white. Ample light again fosters a carefree, intimate attitude; one lattice wall allows sunny patterns to dance in a hallway all day.

The owners of this Manhattan penthouse transformed a warren of small, rooftop maids' rooms into an incandescent aerie. After walls were removed, huge windows installed, and large white floor tiles set in place, the rooms were tinged the merest breath of opalescent pink. The color is not at all perceptible by day, but causes the apartment to blush softly just before night falls.

Happily anticipating her summer visitors, the painter who owns this country house repickles her living-room floor each spring. She freshens the soft draperies and pillows, and arranges her provincial-style furnishings into intimate groupings to encourage conversation. Everything in the room is white to draw attention to her watercolors and shell collection, and to harmonize with the airy porch outside.

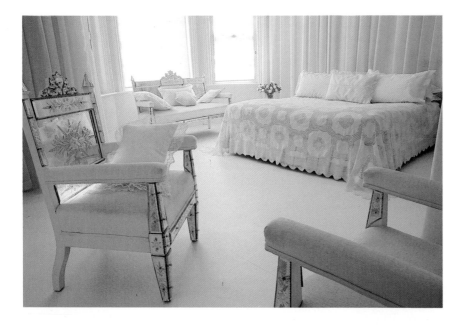

In a *fin-de-siècle* courtyard building in London, fashion designer Jean Muir found a luxuriously proportioned apartment saturated with light. Here she daringly mixed materials—plastic, glossy wood, nubbly fabric, and lace—and furniture ranging from linear to sinuous. All coalesce in white to create a mood at once sophisticated and cozy. In her bedroom, flawlessly crafted Irish linens and laces mantle the bed and cover pillows of various sizes. The mirror-appliquéd chairs and settee once belonged to a maharaja. The furnishings in the living and dining rooms are modular and mobile, conducive to gatherings large or small. The specially designed square tables in the dining room, opposite and overleaf, converge or separate—harmonious for a large dinner party and equally congenial for a luncheon for two.

A jazz singer personally orchestrated the metamorphosis of her raw loft into a spacious yet hospitable home-cum-studio. She built a soaring arch to separate the music area from her living space, and laid soft white carpeting underfoot to add attractive definition to her "home." The kitchen and bath were combined in an alcove alongside. A white-laminated lid drops down over the bathtub to provide counter space, and another lid camouflages the radiator next to her bed. The hand-sewn puffy bedcover and cloud-shaped pillows add a touch of tender whimsy to the bed, while elegant lace panels filter light through the large windows.

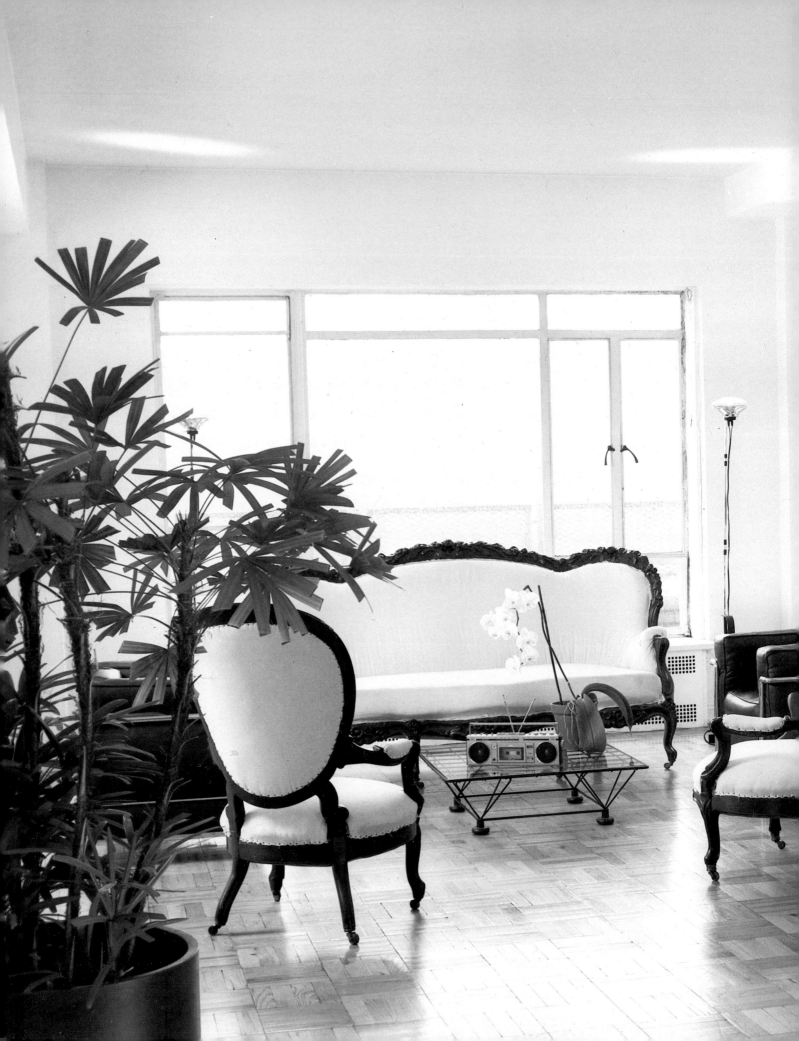

In this high-rise apartment, interior designer William Diamond struck mellifluous harmonies between the serpentine silhouettes of Victorian furnishings and the swell of a grand piano. The sofa and chairs stand out because they are covered in simple, white, nail-studded muslin, left in its unaffected state (and not covered over) because it is charming just as it is. Skinny industrial lighting fixtures at the room's corners beam white moonlike spots onto the ceiling.

Light, white bedrooms, whether lacy or gently tailored, inspire delicious dreams. Opposite: A summer bed really needs no sheets at all, only a wraparound mattress protector and diaphanous canopy. This page, above: Unadorned cotton sheets dramatize the towering French doors in a turn-of-the-century townhouse. Right, top: Furnishings evocative of a 1930s Hollywood movie and flower-flecked white wallpaper lend this sunny bedroom an aura of saucy innuendo. Center: A Parisian boudoir recalls an old-fashioned tableau with its *mélange* of linens, pillows, white flowers, and books. Bottom: The simplest bed is a comforter-topped mattress on the floor; white deck paint invites barefoot ease indoors and out. Overleaf: Thirty floors up, a sleek white lacquered platform elevates a bed to a view of New York's Central Park.

Under the eaves of a recycled Parisian factory building, a tented and fringed bedroom exudes an engagingly exotic atmosphere. Down the stair, the rest of the cavernous space was whitened just as the bedroom was, enabling a jungle of plants to thrive on the reflected light. Wicker chairs and other found objects have been painted white, too, so that the mood of the whole is summery all year round.

For years, Patrizia Anichini sold antique linens and clothes out of her spacious New York loft. At its windowed end, twin swivel chairs, draped with Marseilles spreads, were layered with pieces selected for special display. At the center of the loft, a leopard rug thrown between damask-covered sofas eyed a gilt mannikin. Several tall folding screens, made of wood-framed panels of white cotton, defined areas within the loft and diffused background light.

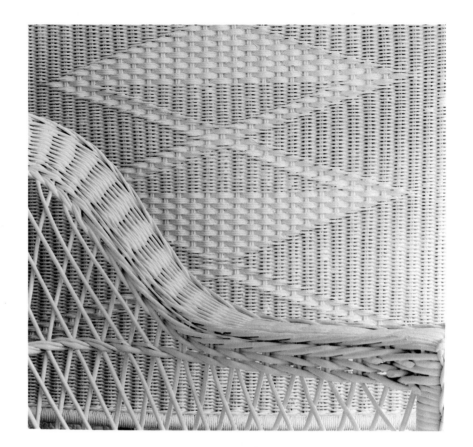

icker saw its heyday in the Victorian era, when conservatories and gardens were arranged with these fanciful yet elegant and often exotic reed furnishings. Frequently wicker pieces, such as these owned by Pamela McGinley Scurry, were painted white to wed their myriad textures and designs. Now back in vogue, wicker's graceful patterns add allure to any room in the house. Opposite: A California couple transplanted their easygoing lifestyle to New England, converting a screened-in porch into an all-white, glass-walled, year-round spa, complete with a white hot-tub, enticing wicker chaise, and tropical plants.

RUSTIC WHITES

radiate a warmth and
unaffected charm

Rustic rooms and rustic houses draw on a tradition in architecture that is ingenuous and matter-of-fact. Every country in the world exhibits its own indigenous solutions to primitive shelter. Although the forms may differ, depending on local materials, tools, and expertise, the basic premise remains constant: to build an economical, suitable, uncomplicated home that will protect its inhabitants from the vagaries of the local climate.

That such dwelling places are often white is readily explained by the wide availability of lime—a cheap, easy-to-work-with material used in producing stucco and plaster. In northern areas, where wood predominates as a building material, stucco fills in and seals the spaces between timbers and coats them thoroughly. Thatch-roofed farmhouses in Ireland and Denmark and half-timbered cottages in England exemplify this type of application. In the Mediterranean, stucco may mantle an entire house, including the roof. The sugar-cube structures found throughout the Greek islands or in Sidi-bou-Zid in Tunisia or in Andalusia in southern Spain are examples of this vernacular architecture.

In America, beginning in the colonial period, wood-frame, clapboard houses have commonly been protected by a thick coat of white paint, which, like plaster, has always been inexpensive and convenient. White farmhouses, Cape Cods, and colonial-style homes persist in many parts of the United States; their forthright appeal suggests a sturdy, unprepossessing American norm.

Today, the warmth and unaffected charm of the "cottage" can be reproduced in country and city rooms alike. Ballasted and structurally defined by woods, which may be dark or pale or even bleached or pickled white, rustic spaces are designed to give a sense of solid reassurance. Here, white plaster is liberally applied to walls and ceiling and may be troweled for a dense, sculptural effect.

The furnishings and accessories that fill these robust spaces frequently show a fundamental appreciation for handicrafts. Hand-hewn, hand-sewn, hand-buffed, tactile pieces, in white, lend each room a wholesome, hearty look.

The fabrics in rustic rooms—be they cottons, linens, or wools—appear homespun. They are fibers that age gracefully, fading in time to a muted off-white or ivory tone. Whether as thin as muslin or as thick as canvas, the fabrics are usually left plain, except for simple stitching that quietly enhances the weave of the cloth. The fine, threaded curlicues decorating a bridal quilt, for example, or the thick warp-and-weft of a raggy rug, honor folk arts and crafts and add a measure of unpretentious loveliness to a rustic decor.

Mixed with baskets, chunky white candles, shutters, or even a slowly swirling ceiling fan that might otherwise hang on a summer porch, these white objects—in the white rooms that surround them—embody an honest spirit. It is a spirit that feigns nothing; a spirit that is winsome, direct, and sincere.

An enormous barn in Connecticut was redesigned by artist Paul Leonard to appear both provincial and theatrical. In the immense living room/atelier, the walls, chimneypiece, and beams are all thickly coated with whitewash to enhance textures and amplify light. In summer, the fireplace cavity receives a lick of whitewash, too, for visual "cool," and birch logs are placed inside. The owners combined their overscaled white sofa, draped with a loosely woven afghan, with white painted pieces to calm the mix of shapes and sizes. The master bedroom features an iron bedstead, capped with a tray-top raw silk canopy, and pale sisal matting on the floor.

Overleaf: At one end of a narrow all-white bath in a reconstructed barn in upstate New York, a huge, gleaming porcelain tub offers bathers a relaxing view of trees and sky.

When Redroof Design, architects, built a greenhouse to connect a barn to a cobbler's cottage, they unified the structures with a judicious dose of white paint. By this means, they also reconciled dissimilar windows. The interior walls and duck upholstery (and bath fixtures salvaged from a hotel) were also coordinated in white.

As part of the refurbishing of a 1940s adobe house in Santa Fe, thickset walls were pierced by big multi-paned windows. The interiors throughout were then painted white to capitalize on the new infusion of light. White, cotton-covered furnishings emphasize the sculptural simplicity of the interiors.

A thatch-roofed, stucco-clad farmhouse in the Danish countryside offers a comfortable weekend retreat for a citybound family. One room casually rambles on to the next, and then through Dutch doors to the grassy patio outside. The furniture, an offbeat amalgam of wicker and wood, harmonizes because everything is white. White, frosted-glass pendants spotlight the dining table and work counters in the kitchen.

ood armatures and special woven furnishings come alive by being a juxtaposition with white in four country living rooms. Opposite: White planking sets off the skeleton of an English timbered barn reconstructed on Long Island, and white furnishings settle into the space without distracting from its impressive scale. This page, top: In a country house in France, big white pillows replace conventional seating. An open-tread wooden stair leading to the upper floor looks sculptural in this simple setting. Center: The interior of a small Nantucket cottage, designed by Billy Baldwin, seems larger because of the whitened walls, mantle, and rugs. White canvas covers the designer's signature chairs. Bottom: A California beach house, designed by Michael Taylor, gets a big dollop of coziness from pale, oversized straw furniture and plump white cushions.

In a sprawling New York City apartment overlooking Gramercy Park, the urban sophistication of sleek armless seating mingles skillfully with the charm of warm woods, pottery, and baskets. A dramatic white folding screen shields the doorway to the master bedroom, where a white ceiling fan swirls breezes over the platform bed. Right and overleaf: A functional collection of chunky white hotel and restaurant china makes a sculptural display on tables and shelves.

The radiance of white in these simply furnished bedrooms, buffered by rustic woods, fabrics, and stone, captures the freshness and peacefulness of the country. Opposite: In her own New York City bedroom, decorator Alexandra Stoddard added the rural touches of rag rugs, wicker, and a scallop-edged bridal quilt. All are pure white. This page, top: On the Greek island of Lindos, white river pebbles pave the floor of a sea captain's bedroom, complementing the simple cotton bedcover and iron bedstead. Bottom: To make a tiny cottage bedroom appear more spacious, interior designer William Walter repeated the white of the plastered walls on the painted sleigh bed and its linens, and angled the bed in the center of the room to give more space all around.

Massachusetts caterer Bobbie Crosby selected pure white for the kitchen in her renovated house—a former roadstop and inn—because its neutrality allows her to visualize the colorful impact of the dishes she prepares. Subtly veined white marble countertops and provincial-style painted wood cabinets set off the primitive antiques and heavy-duty cookware.

64

aymond Waites uses his white getaway house as a testing ground for household products such as giant white nesting bowls and flower-dappled white bed linens that he designs. Waites also likes a neutral environment for displaying his collection of country pine furniture and finds that even dead *ficus* trees become ornamental here. Overleaf: A little window punched into the living-room wall adds a note of whimsy, especially with a miniature flock of woolly white sheep roaming the sill.

REFINED WHITES

express confidence
and sophisticated grace

White, in design, has often been equated with an elevated level of taste and grace, an ideal. Aristocratic and refined in concept, the ideal connotes a polished, sophisticated manner that is always courtly and polite. White, in this guise, permits no lowering of standards. Even the most daring combination of the proper and the outrageous, when used in a refined room, moves beyond the merely trendy to the sublime. In a refined room, every detail is selected for its innate purity and integrity; every element blends beautifully each with the next and with the setting as a whole. Once this harmony is achieved, the room radiates a confidence that is symphonic in tone and elegant in manner.

One version of the refined ideal is the legacy of Greek and Roman architecture and its classical vocabulary—columns, pilasters, pediments, and the like—which has been employed for centuries to lend a dignity and majesty to civic buildings, churches, and stately homes in Europe and the United States. This classical vocabulary has been complemented, at various times, with stucco work, which seems at first glance to be pure confection; however, closer examination reveals a craftsmanship conceived to enhance a refined decor.

A new, airier refinement in white came at the turn of this century in the evocative furniture created by architect-designer Charles Rennie Mackintosh in Scotland and by Eliel Saarinen in Finland. Their white furnishings were coordinated with carefully composed room settings to present a lyrical and calm environment. At the same time, in America, decorator Elsie de Wolfe transformed gloomy Victorian interiors with "plenty of optimism and white paint," furnishing her interiors with pale or white pieces for a lighter, gayer mood.

During the 1930s, white-on-white reached new heights—in the rooms of England's Syrie Maugham. Her amalgam of furnishings and accessories, considered shocking at the time, fueled a new look that combined the prosaic with the *outré* in one grand, opulent sweep of white. She brought together feathers and leathers, furs and shells, mirrors and glass, to create a setting that was urbane and exciting.

Today, refined rooms enjoy this same tension between elements. In white, the mix works best when the surrounding shell is impeccable. Paint, therefore, is often applied with painstaking artistry to achieve the unblemished luster of fine porcelain. Ceramic tiles or marble, used on walls or floors, are so installed as to appear seamless and may be buffed to perfect their complexion.

In refined rooms, fabrics are chosen for their superb quality: gossamer silks and polished cottons, rich damasks and brocades, or perhaps near-translucent handkerchief linens. These fabrics are controlled in their drape, hung with an unerring eye to proportion. Upholstery, inventive yet precise, displays a dressmaker's flair for detail.

The atmosphere of refined rooms is always gracious, secure, balanced, and correct. In scale, in texture, in the quality of light, and, above all, in their feeling of assured self-awareness, refined rooms strive for perfection in every way.

lamour, luxury, and drama were the three prerequisites presented to designer Ronald Bricke for a room to be used solely for entertaining. Bricke opted for a snow-white space, to float between two deep-hued rooms. Facing walls became sculptures: The window wall, built out to conceal the heating/cooling system and stereo speakers, also contains banks of theatrical footlights, which play multiple patterns of light and color throughout the room; the fireplace overmantel was molded especially for this space by sculptor Louis Lieberman, then fixed in place with plaster.

A once-dark, wood-paneled duplex apartment was transformed into an immense, sun-saturated white oasis by interior designer Angelo Donghia for Ralph Lauren, the fashion and home furnishings entrepreneur, and his wife, Ricky. The Laurens wanted to start decorating anew in this home, and Donghia provided them with pure space that would evolve as they added furniture, art, and sculpture. He also gave them the perfect accessories for an oasis: big, comfortable rattan and linen seating, huge broad-leafed plants, and giant baskets—all of which suit the superb dimensions of the space. In all rooms, deeply recessed windows provide "dioramic" views of the city.

Overleaf: Honoring the majestic proportions and classical moldings of a monumental reception room in a Manhattan townhouse, designer Noel Jeffrey united all elements, including contemporary seating of his own design, in one grand sweep of white.

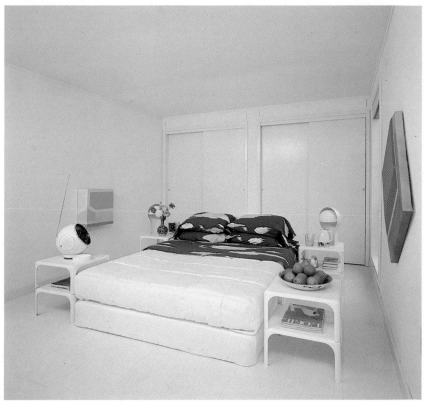

This plain, prefabricated modular house on an unassuming plot gained stature and sophistication through gracious attention to detail, and a brilliant coat of white paint inside and out. A glassed-in entry/dining area links the modules, and all interior spaces are thus liberated from any feeling of constriction. The white-on-white palette is continued in the furnishings, many of which were imported from Italy. Portable, but still elegant, the plastic pieces welcome company, and may be gathered together at a moment's notice.

Voluptuous furnishings reminiscent of those found on ocean liners during their heyday fill a suave *pied-à-terre*
designed by the team Bray-Schaible.
Special padded wainscoting, wrapped
in resilient monochromatic luggage nylon, adorns both the living room and the
adjacent bedroom. Thick chenille welt-
ing softens the lines of the shipboard-
style easy chairs; the pillows ranging
along the living room banquette are also
fringed. Enormous lacquered-wood
trays function as tabletops.

In his simply furnished Helsinki apartment, industrial designer Ristomatti Ratia simultaneously finds repose and a place to generate new ideas. White, he feels, best inspires his thinking. Against a pure white surround, Ratia consciously mixes Finnish antiques with glossy metal contemporary pieces. One of his own first designs, the Palaset system of boxes functions as a pedestal for an old cupboard.

At every turn, Ratia's apartment reveals neat, elegantly conceived vignettes combining old and new, color and white, rough texture and smooth. Stripped pine doors, hand-thrown pottery, crinkled paper—all stand out against white. The kitchen is clearly organized: White kitchenwares of many shapes mix compatibly on open shelves. White wicker chairs, a whiff of country, flank the simple kitchen table.

Italian architect Claudio Dini indulged many tactile impressions in this urbane apartment—shimmering floor tile, sheer lace, slick metal, and slubby fabric—all in white. The interaction of these textures forms a resonant counterpoint to prized collections of leatherbound books and old paintings.

Overleaf: To enhance a mood of opulence in David Hicks's Paris showroom, designer Christian Badin bound a wall of books in thick white vellum.

91

The metamorphoses of three quite different New York living rooms were accomplished through a polished use of white, transforming the scale and character of each from banal to elegant. Opposite: Decorator Stephanie Stokes dispelled the gloom of her dark, enormously high-ceilinged studio by painting the brown walls white and introducing satiny white seating and a mirrored screen. This page, top: To enliven a living room, designer Ronald Bricke painted white checks on the parquet floor and used glass cabinets and prisms to beam light patterns onto white walls, ceiling, and furnishings. Bottom: The design team Hutchings-Lyle placed twin white sofas at a casual diagonal to extenuate the architectural boxiness of this high-rise apartment. Vertical blinds provide a jazzy note against horizontal windows.

Overleaf: Unusual vellum-covered side chairs by Karl Springer are an esoteric complement to a naive pine table.

Gossamer white cotton scrims tethered to floor and ceiling tracks were devised by tapestry designer Bruce Bierman to separate the living and sleeping spaces in his loft. Strings of tiny white Christmas lights glow along a window sill all year.

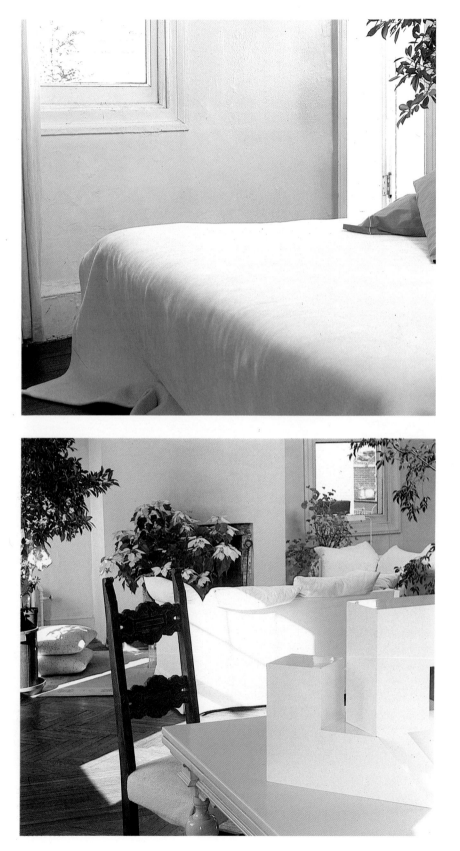

ree of inhibiting clutter, an artist's penthouse appears almost monas-
tic in its simplicity. In the living room,
white furnishings are minimal but
comfortable, placed precisely to offset
modular white sculptures. Trees
breathe freshness into both the living
room and the bedroom and beckon to
the terraces outside. In the bath, the
only color comes from the glimmer of a
solid brass pyramid balanced on the
edge of the tub.

journalist who covers the arts in her professional life retires to a simple, unaffected white space to refresh her thoughts, enjoy music, and write. With an astute eye to proportion and balance, she made no effort to camouflage the dowager building's moldings and trim, but instead integrated structure and seating through white.

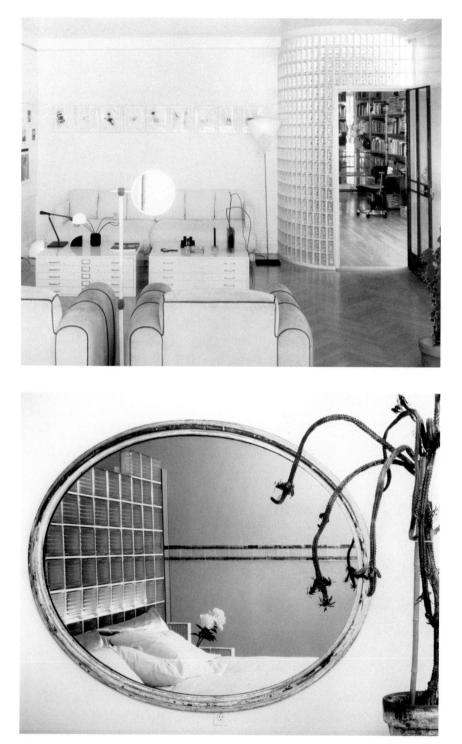

Adapting a number of industrial materials, such as glass blocks and metal-framed doors, to the renovation of a spacious Manhattan apartment, architect Alan Buchsbaum imbued the space with cultured sparkle. The glass allows inner rooms to borrow light from outer ones. The placement of an unpretentious oval mirror in the bedroom attracts even more light. Low, white flat files, used as coffee tables and for storage, take on a rare beauty.

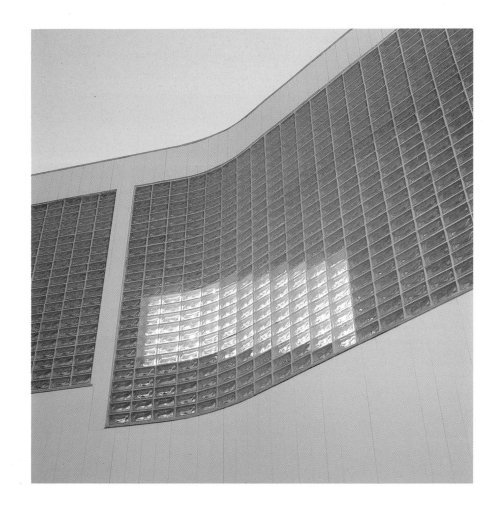

RATIONAL WHITES

reveal the logic
of functional design

Calculated, ordered, and precise, the design for a rational room or house is predicated on the rigorous interpretation of a concise architectural vocabulary. This vocabulary may involve classical precepts, taken literally or transmuted into humorous or theatrical statements; alternatively, it may be derived from combinations of basic formal geometries—specifically the square and the cube, and to a lesser degree the circle and the triangle.

This preoccupation with a pure building geometry—devoid of ornament and extraneous detailing—is a particularly twentieth-century phenomenon. Its theoretical underpinnings received their first enunciation in the unadorned cubic volumes conceived by architect Adolf Loos in such houses as his Villa Steiner in Vienna. The principles continued to be streamlined and refined in the architecture of the Bauhaus and of Le Corbusier.

The Bauhaus exalted the glory of industrial technology and the new mass production of precision building materials such as steel and glass. It thus liberated architecture from its swaddling of masonry to establish tensile and elegant skeletal frameworks that would permit interiors to flow freely and be saturated with light. Interior partitions, usually white, amplified the sense of spaciousness and allowed light to magnify and refract within. Mies van der Rohe applied the Bauhaus concept in the United States, creating spare, white-clad steel-and-glass houses that dramatized the idea of shelter at its most abstract.

Le Corbusier, with houses such as his Villa Savoie near Paris, inspired countless disciples both in the United States and elsewhere. In Le Corbusier's vision, a house such as the Villa Savoie, isolated in its purity and whiteness, invited an intellectual and emotional response to nature at its most elemental: light and air became absolutes necessary to energy and life.

With the Bauhaus and Le Corbusier, the pure expression of function within a shelter was unencumbered by ornamental distractions; today, as then, function is the key to rational design. White in a rational space underscores the logic of functional design, whether in a solar-heated greenhouse, where white-painted surfaces harness light, or in a kitchen where white highlights the compact efficiency of the work area and equipment.

Honest, unprepossessing white materials, man-made or natural, are put to use with exacting dexterity and with no exaggeration in rational rooms. Carpeting is unpretentious and even in texture; upholstery, of plain materials and solid weaves, tends to be pulled taut and left untrimmed. All is disciplined and in control.

Whiteness simply and unequivocally clarifies the vivid architectural juxtapositions that occur in a rational room: volume to void; surface to space; flat plane to sculptural mass. Although rational design may sometimes appear cerebral and purposefully spare, it is never antiseptic. As we witness the integration of light with space and of form with texture, we become aware not only of the engineering of architecture, but of the art of architecture as well.

The meticulously articulated houses of architect Richard Meier's *oeuvre* are cool, crisp structures that stand out in sharp contrast to their landscape. At the same time, however, these houses express a deeply cherished American dream: the flawless fusion of indoors and out. Meier accomplishes this through his studied concentration on white juxtaposed with glass; there is no beginning nor end to white as it moves across, around, and through his houses. Overleaf: Meier likes light to sweep through his interiors, as in this chaste and highly disciplined Connecticut living room.

112

113

German architect and industrial designer Dieter Rams built his compact, Bauhaus-inspired home to permit flexibility in furniture placement. Rams designed a latticework of grids through windows, cabinetry, and floor tiles. Set against the geometry of these grids, the curvaceous lines of nineteenth-century bentwoods appear almost voluptuous.

116

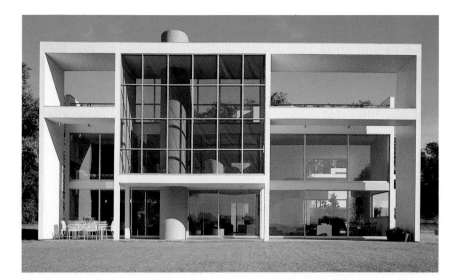

A rigorously conceived Mondrianesque house near Cincinnati, by architects Charles Gwathmey and Robert Siegel, is firmly rooted in a carpet of grass. Inside, the architects dispelled any temptation to focus on the formal lines of the structure by thrusting an undulating hallway through the house. A study is at one end of the hallway, and at the other stands a companionable seating area, opposite. White walls in this space support glass brick inlays, which harness light and work well with straw, oak, and other natural textures.

White in five different kitchens adds drama and heightens the feeling of space. Opposite: A slick white breakfast bar increases the capabilities of a galley kitchen designed by Chicago architect Marvin Ullman. This page, top left: White unifies appliances and cabinets (even baseboard drawers) in a small German kitchen. Top right: A free-standing white "box" defines a modern country kitchen designed by Mariette Himes Gomez. Bottom left: A narrow white kitchen unit blends unobtrusively in an office setting. Bottom right: Against dark floor tiles, a curved white work island looks clean and sculptural in architect Charles Morris Mount's design.

Fashion designer Adri asked interior designer Kevin Walz to create a pristine white health spa within her Manhattan loft. At the center of the space, Walz raised a platform for a pool outfitted with massaging jets. The platform and pool are blanketed in white tiles, angled for architectural interest.

122

ouses utilizing principles of passive solar energy require a carefully balanced ratio of light-reflective, often white, surfaces to light-absorbent, dark materials in order to maximize the benefits of the sun's rays. Opposite: A trussed skylight system by architect Alfredo de Vido invigorates a living room in New Jersey; shades pull over the glass panes on cloudy days and at night to retain collected heat. This page, top: Architect Paul Rudolph devoted an entire wall of a grandly scaled house to its heat-absorbing greenhouse. Center: In Connecticut, an indoor pool, also by de Vido, is warmed by skylights and glass-paned walls facing south-southwest. Bottom: A heat-snaring glass porch designed by William Ellis appears to float across the back of a New England clapboard house, fusing new and old architectural elements.

124

The white-clapboarded formality of a colonial American telescope house is recaptured in this witty contemporary version by architect Hugh Newell Jacobson. Jacobson assigned each segment in the telescope a specific function—living room, entry, and so on. While ground-floor windows remain constant in size, upper-story windows gradually disappear under the descending roofline. The narrow end of the house, opposite, reveals that glass panels fill the spaces between segments, endowing the interiors with extra light and glimpses of the out-of-doors.

On a great swath of Kentucky bluegrass, Hugh Newell Jacobson sited a temple-like house boasting eighty-six white columns and a sweeping white crushed-marble drive. Since the location is remote, privacy was not a concern, and the all-white interior spaces move one into the next with no doorways to interrupt the conceptual flow. In the living room, white linen-cloaked sofas and near-invisible tables form conversation islands; the travertine floor reaches past the outer glass walls to the colonnades. Overleaf: The house surveys its land in all directions from atop a marble-faced pedestal.

inspire introspection
and creative thought

Certain singular spaces evoke images so personal they defy classification. It is to such places—rarefied rooms—that this chapter is dedicated. Rarefied rooms affect us in the same way as a mirage might; they mesmerize with allusion and illusion until we become unsure of what is real and what is not quite real. Rarefied rooms enjoin us to contemplate reality itself and encourage us to question the feelings, associations, and dreams that subliminally alter our understanding of reality.

In particular revered places, our perceptions of the worldly and the divine merge. The Taj Mahal, shining white at the end of a long pool, tantalizes us with a radiant appreciation of both the minute and the monumental. A Japanese garden, composed of white pebbles raked into meticulous patterns, transcends the very stones that define its temporal state and challenges us to arrive at another level of consciousness.

For some people today, a sense of identity cannot be clothed in ordinary garb or contained within ordinary rooms. To a visitor, these living spaces necessarily appear enigmatic and sometimes aloof, outside concrete definitions. An ordinary loft space, for instance, transformed from its origin as a sweatshop into an art gallery, may become in itself a work of art. An ordinary high-rise apartment might, with special lighting effects, become an incandescent theater for make-believe.

Whiteness in rarefied rooms softens actual dimensions, diffusing edges so that they lead into an indefinite beyond. When fabrics such as rip-stop nylon or simple cotton sheeting are used to shroud rooms or drape furniture, their softness and swag create shapes seemingly without substance.

When light enters a rarefied room, it does so obliquely; it appears evasive and elusive, filtered or diverted for dramatic effect. Sometimes shutters or blinds reroute the light, breaking it into startling bands of hot white and cool shadow. Sometimes translucent panels of fabric or plastic veil the light source, muting its impact and encouraging hallucinatory images. And sometimes the light emanates solely from an unexpected source—a television screen perhaps—and this light, too, alters our perception of the room.

Rarefied rooms inspire introspection and creative thought: meditation, dreaming, reading, writing—all are intense experiences here. Rarefied rooms fuse reality and fantasy; they are real, surreal, supernally real.

A gallery owner painted everything in his gallery loft white as a luminescent ground for exhibiting large-scale artworks in a variety of media. In doing so, he also transformed commonplace furnishings—cast-off office chairs and tables made from doors set on trolley wheels—into beautiful "art-i-facts," relieving them of their previous mundane associations.

138

The serene understatement of the Japanese aesthetic is achieved in this cavernous loft space furnished only with plain white tufted futons and an outsized paper lantern. Careful placement of stones, a pottery bowl—even a simple hand-thrown tea service—within this white space allows these objects to be observed in their unblemished purity. Goldfish swim in the curved pool, foreground, that echoes the arch of the fireplace cavity.

ofts are often whitened not only to emphasize their scale and openness, but to distance them spiritually from their origins as sweatshops and warehouses. This page: Designer Mark Hulla constructed an austere cellblock for a trio of bed cubicles in a loft, then played fantasy games with a false window, checkerboard floor, and skinny banners. Opposite, top: Architect William Meyer introduced a special white module into a large loft to confine the area devoted to cooking and dining. Bottom: In this spare loft, seating was achieved by pulling pillows off a stack and arranging them into various configurations.

Overleaf: A serene still life is a study in tone and texture, displaying an artful juxtaposition of pebble and pearl.

143

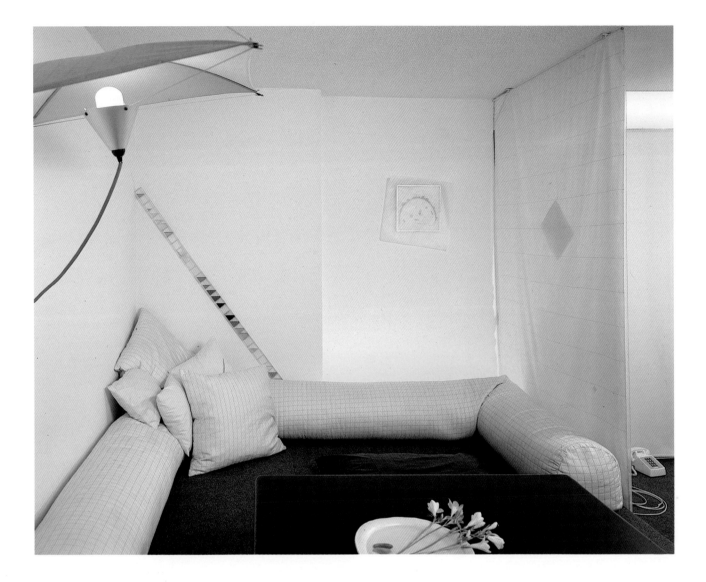

In their home-studio, textile designers Nob + Non struck a subtle balance between minimal furnishings and art objects of their own creation. Translucent white fabric panels screen the conversation platform from the work area; another fabric remnant, opposite, veils a bedroom lamp.

transitory draping can transmute rooms into sculptures, enjoyable for their very evanescence and for the otherworldliness they evoke. This page: A reading corner becomes a three-dimensional work of art through the use of yards of Belgian linen; designers Allan Scruggs and Douglas Myers gathered some on the floor, then slipped extra strips over furnishings and through a slatted blind. Opposite, top: Artist Diana Carulli's "Dreamboats"—fabricated from white rip-stop nylon—function as environmental sculptures but also as projection screens on which filmed images hover and glow. Bottom: Designers Antonio Morello and Donato Savoie of New York's Studio Morsa wrapped and tied the furniture in a tented dining room for a phantasmagoric bacchanal. Overleaf: A ghostly living room subsides beneath dropcloths in artist-photographer Uwe Ommer's home.

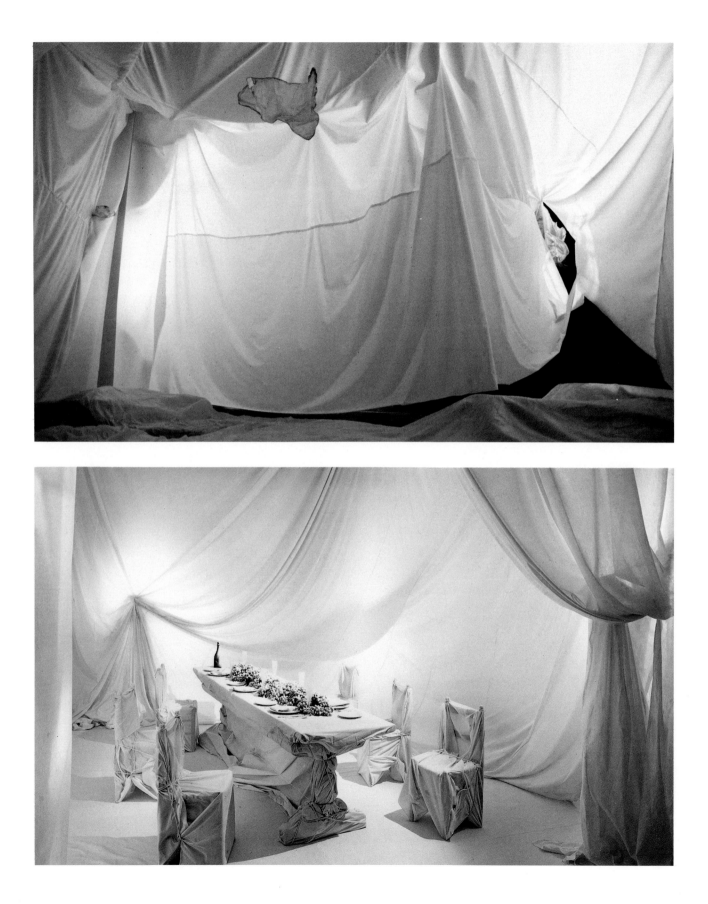

What might have been an ordinary Manhattan apartment is instead a theater for animated lighting effects played off against white walls. Designers Dennis di Lorenzo and Mario loCicero came up with an ingenious solution for the nonworking fireplace: Fire gives way to the movement of light and water. A specially designed backlit tank—coursed with bubbles—now fills the fireplace cavity. Overhead, under palm fronds, pinspot lights beam colored "Miami" moons.

Two white offices exhibit unusual and highly individualized decors. Opposite: Architect Elizabeth McClintock designed a showroom environment seemingly frozen in time, plugged into the everyday only by a telephone. Above: Time seems to fly in a studio designed by Michael Haskins which is lit by a white plastic pear.

155

Outside fluctuations of leaf and light become an ongoing work of art in an otherwise white-on-white suburban bedroom designed by Charles Damga. To banish any air of sterility from the space, he added fakes and whimsies: a fireplace that could never be lit, a violin that would never be played, and columns that support nothing.

An apartment in Barcelona, introspective and inscrutable in its very whiteness, bears its furnishings with virtually no allusion to traditional notions of comfort. Chairs and tables relate directly to the works of art in the open spaces, not to each other. The art, by contrast, mocks this studious, almost ascetic composure, revealing an inner exuberance and wit.

Overleaf: A slender white meditation cell, open on four sides, glows quietly in a dark room designed for yoga and exercise by architect Gamal el Zoghby.

158

In a contemporary high-rise apartment, boxes of white vinyl tiles, bought to conceal dark parquet floors, were found mistakenly to come in two tones, so they were installed throughout the living room and kitchen as a subtle checkerboard. To eliminate the need for standard lamps, two huge lightbox tables were built; the twist of a rheostat transforms the mood of the room from sunny to subdued. Music speakers are clad in the same white canvas as the pillowed seating.

A family that lives on Staten Island wanted the visual experience of living outdoors year-round and opted for an all-white scheme to call to mind a front-porch nearness to nature. Minimizing upkeep was a concern, too, so floors were tiled in marbleized vinyl. Upholstery is also vinyl. Two white-painted picnic tables sit side by side in the kitchen. Overleaf: Shutters throughout the house add to the fresh-air feeling, and silk flowers perpetuate a springtime mood.

165

RESORT WHITES

rejuvenate and
set the spirit free

The idea of resort is simple and salutary: to feel relaxed and renewed, we must celebrate the immediate, uninhibited satisfaction of appetite, companionship, and rest in a place that makes us feel good. A resort may be a whitewashed condominium facing a summery sea, or it may be a spanking-clean wooden deck surrounding a backyard pool. But whatever it is, it bids us forget the regimen of the everyday, allows us to indulge our need for pure, unhurried pleasure, and frees us to receive all sensations with delight.

Resort rooms, in white, take a cue from the tropics, where for years white plaster and white paint have been used to rebuff heat, diffuse light, and foster a feeling of carefree ease. The white porch or veranda, the white patio or terrace: these places encourage refreshment in locales as diverse as Bermuda or Haiti or Mexico.

Resort rooms are blithe of spirit and buoyant of mood. They cry out, "Bare your feet! Bare your legs! Bare your head!" They rejoice in tactile sensation. The granular texture of sand is expressed in crunchy white cottons and linens; the sheen of water is duplicated in the slick glaze of ceramic tiles or again in the gleam of marine deck paint; the froth of surf is captured in the fragile folds of a net canopy that drops around a bed or in the soothing softness of a terry towel.

Many resort rooms open directly to the outside. Walls enclose only when they must for privacy. In cold climates rooms fully enwrap for coziness, and, in white, they radiate a fire's warmth or a candle's beguiling flame while affording a feeling of freedom and release.

Resort rooms encourage improvisation. Furnishings tend to be portable: pads, pillows, and mattresses, which may serve for sunning or lounging or sleeping, are meant to be manipulated at will. To be maintenance-free, resort upholstery is designed free of trimmings and other adornments; these pieces are often made simply, in natural fabrics, such as cotton, which bleach still whiter if left outdoors.

Casual and congenial, resort rooms rejuvenate us. Whether fired with hedonistic longings or tranquilly anticipating repose, we feel absolved of care in these places of renewal and attuned to our innermost energies.

A fashion designer's vacation retreat near St. Tropez integrates the pale, smooth stone indigenous to the region with great expanses of glass in a relaxed open-plan scheme. The white canvas pads stacked in the living room were devised to offer countless options for lounging. A huge umbrella, also white canvas, shelters a casual outdoor dining table.

Two white living rooms—one geared to summer living and the other designed for a wintry clime—exhibit differing perspectives on leisure, but similar notions of comfort. Above: In southern Italy, ease of upkeep is essential near the sea; it is enhanced in this room by the fact that storage and seating (and a fireplace for cool nights) have all been molded directly from the white stucco structure to form one continuous unit. Pillows flesh out the platforms, and straw trays act as portable tables. Right: A white room in Canada is rendered cozy and inviting by the glow reflected from a compact wood stove.

Overleaf: Designer Waldo Fernandez tossed a collection of colorful "beachball" pillows into a sun-baked California beachfront bedroom, using their dazzle as a bracing contrast to his otherwise white scheme.

176

oft sand and shell tones warm the interiors of an island vacation house off the coast of North Carolina and blend unobtrusively with the dunes just outside. The living level is totally open, room to room, taking advantage of ocean and inlet views on all sides.

In the Dominican Republic, Mexican architect Marco Aldaco created an escapist's dream complex composed of thatch-roofed structures called "palapas." Some of the spaces are open, since this island is relatively bug free, and some, for privacy, are enclosed. All walls were sculpted of clay thickly sealed with white plaster, and appointments such as banquettes, bathing tubs, shower stalls, and mirror inserts were molded by hand from the same material.

esigner Barbara Littman created an easy-care atmosphere in a big, rambling Victorian house on the New Jersey shore by limiting furnishings to a set of white folding camp chairs, a plastic cylindrical table, and a pile of soft pillows that beckon guests to relax anywhere they want.

185

A stark skeletal frame, designed by Detroit architect Dino Rossetti, outlines a pool and patio in Florida and captures views of sky, sunset, and water beyond.

186

Against the rugged volcanic backdrop of the Canary Islands, a painter and his wife created a whitewashed house and studio that tame the surrounding landscape. Outdoor terraces reach out to embrace stones, lava formations, and island vegetation. One terrace is for dining, another encloses a pool; on a third, white chaises invite stretching out in the sun.

Overleaf: White decking completely wraps around a brilliant blue pool in East Hampton and smoothly frames its scatter-patterned reflections.

EPILOGUE

Once upon a time, there was a dream place, and it was a white room. The floor canted in the white room, and the walls splayed out. Slender hanging ladders and catwalks intersected the space. There were doors that opened and shut in the white room, and when they were shut the room's surface always returned to a seamless continuity.

Into the dream place, men and women entered. They ran, they climbed, they swung, and they danced. They spoke, and they fell in love. When they spoke, the poetry of their words unfurled, engaged, melted, clung, and lived fiercely. The men and the women in the dream place evolved from shadows into everything they could possibly be. Agile, balletic, poetic, silly, they became full with the urgency of language and living. The dream place, the white room, contained but never confined, reached to infinities and infinite hope.

COMPANY ADDRESSES

Every effort was made to ensure the accuracy of the information contained in this catalogue. However, with time, addresses and names do change, so a compilation of this sort cannot, despite all efforts, be absolutely precise.

ALLIBERT BATH
Bath accessories
3428A Vane Court
Charlotte, NC 28206
(800) 346-2428

ALLIBERT OUTDOOR FURNITURE
1200 Hwy. 27 South
Stanley, NC 28164

AMERICAN STANDARD, INC.
Bath accessories
1114 Ave. of the Americas
New York, NY 10036
(212) 708-5484

ARCONAS CORP.
Upholstery, outdoor
580 Orwell St.
Mississauga, Ontario
Canada L5A 3V7
(416) 272-0727

ARFLEX SpA
Upholstery, storage
Via Monte Rosa 27
22051 Limbiate
Milan
Italy

Neil Rogers Interiors
Unit 23 Abbeyville Mews
88 Clatham Park Road
London SW4 7BX
UK
44 (71) 498 1911

ARTEMIDE
Occasional, lighting
Artemide Inc.
30-30 Thompson Ave.
Long Island City, NY 11101
(718) 786-8200

Artemide Ltd.
17/19 Neal Street
Covent Garden
London WC2H 9PU
UK
44 (71) 8366 753

Artemide SpA
Corso Monforte 19
20122 Milan
Italy

ARZBERG
Dinnerware
See Hutschenreuther

AVERY-BOARDMAN LTD.
Upholstery
979 Third Ave.
New York, NY 10022
(212) 688-6611

B & B ITALIA USA INC.
Upholstery
B & B Italia USA Inc.
30-20 Thompson Ave.
IDCNY, 4th Floor
Long Island City, NY 11101
(718) 784-0211

B & B Italia SpA
Strada Provinciale 32
22060 Novodrate (Como)
Italy

Keith de la Plain
Milroy House
5 Sayers Lane
Tenterden
TN 30 6 BW Kent
UK

BAKER, KNAPP & TUBBS
Upholstery
Baker, Knapp & Tubbs
Furniture, Inc.
6-187 Merchandise Mart
Chicago, IL 60654
(312) 337-7144

BENJAMIN & MEDWIN, INC.
Kitchenware
230 Fifth Ave.
New York, NY 10001
(212) 686-0600

BERNARDAUD LIMOGES
Dinnerware
Bernardaud Limoges, N.A.
41 Madison Ave.
New York, NY 10010
(212) 696-2431

Bernardaud Limoges
11 rue Royale
75008 Paris
France
33 (147) 42 82 66

BIEFFE
Occasional
See Sam Flax

BING & GRØNDAHL
Dinnerware. kitchenware
See Royal Copenhagen

BLACK & DECKER
Small appliances, bath accessories
6 Armstrong Rd.
Shelton, CT 06484
(203) 926-3000

BLOCK CHINA CORP.
Dinnerware
11 East 26th St.
New York, NY 10010
(212) 686-7440

BOYD LIGHTING CO.
Lighting
56 Twelfth St.
San Francisco, CA 94103
(415) 431-4300

BRAUN
Small appliances
66 Broadway
Linfield, MA 01940
(617) 592-3300

Braun AG
22 Ruesselsheimer
Frankfurt Main
D-6000
Germany

Braun Electric
Dolphin Estate
Windmill Road
Sunbury-on-Thames
Middlesex TW16 TEJ
UK
44 (9) 3278 5611

BRAYTON INTERNATIONAL COLLECTION
Upholstery, storage
255 Swathmore Ave.
P.O. Box 7288
High Point, NC 27264
(919) 434-4151

BROWN JORDAN
Outdoor
Subsid. of Ladd Furniture Inc.
Box 5688
El Monte, CA 91734
(818) 443-8971

CASA STRADIVARI, INC.
Occasional
221 McKibben St.
Brooklyn, NY 11206
(718) 386-0048

CASTELLI
Occasional
Castelli SpA
Via Torreggiani 1
40128 Bologna
Italy
39 (51) 527 111

Castelli (UK) Ltd.
316-318 Regent St.
London W1
UK
44 (71) 323 3320

CHINA SEAS/HOMEPORT
Kitchenware
Div. of China Seas, Inc.
152 Madison Ave.
Suite 1400
New York, NY 10016
(212) 420-1170

CLAIRITEX
Outdoor
See Allibert Outdoor Furniture

COALPORT
Dinnerware
See Waterford/Wedgwood USA

COGGIN, THAYER
Upholstery, occasional, storage
See Thayer Coggin, Inc.

COPCO
Storage, kitchenware
Copco, a Wilton Industries Co.
2240 West 75th St.
Woodridge, IL 60517
(708) 963-7100

CORNING INC.
Dinnerware, kitchenware
Corning, NY 14831
(607) 974-4261

CREUSET, LE
Kitchenware
Le Creuset
P.O. Box 575
Yemassee, SC 29945
(803) 589-6211

Le Creuset
14 Boulevard Poissonniere
75009 Paris
France

CUISINART CORP.
Small appliances
1 Cummings Pt. Rd.
Stamford, CT 06904
(203) 975-4600

DANSK
Dinnerware
Dansk International
Designs, Ltd.
Radio Circle Rd.
Mt. Kisco, NY 10549
(914) 666-2121

DELTA FAUCET CO.
Bath accessories
Div. of Masco Corp. of Indiana
55 East 111 St.
Indianapolis, IN 46280
(317) 848-1812

DIRECTIONAL OF NORTH
CAROLINA, INC.
Upholstery
P.O. Box 2005
High Point, NC 27261
(919) 841-3209

EKORNES
Storage
Ekornes Inc.
3100 Woodbridge Ave.
Edison, NJ 08837
(908) 225-8660

J.E. Ekornes AS
6222 Ikornnes
Norway

Ekornes Ltd.
St. George's House
12B St. George's Street
London W1
UK
44 (71) 629 6554

Ekornes Sweden
P.O. Box 117
S551 13 Jönköping
Sweden

ELEGANCE INC.
Outdoor
819 North Main St.
High Point, NC 27262
(919) 884-5733

EMU
Emu Gardentime Ltd.
Graveney Road
Faversham
Kent ME13 8UN
UK
44 (7) 95 53 5511

FITZ & FLOYD
Dinnerware
Fitz & Floyd, Inc.
P.O. Box 815367
Dallas, TX 75381
(214) 484-9494

GENERAL HOUSEWARES
CORP.
Kitchenware
P.O. Box 4066
1536 Beech St.
Terre Haute, IN 47804
(812) 232-1000

GEORGE KOVACS
LIGHTING, INC.
Lighting
330 East 59th St.
New York, NY 10022
(212) 838-3400

HALO LIGHTING
Lighting
Div. of Cooper Lighting
400 Busse Rd.
Elk Grove Village, IL 60007
(708) 956-8400

HAMILTON BEACH INC.
Small appliances
4420 Waterfront Dr.
Glen Allen, VA 23060
(414) 273-4680

HANSON SCALE CO.
Bath accessories
Div. of Sunbeam Corp.
Hwy. 45 North
Manning, MI 29102
(800) 621-8854

HASTINGS TILE & IL BAGNO
COLLECTION
Bath accessories
404 Northern Blvd.
Great Neck, NY 11021
(516) 482-1840

HAVILAND LIMOGES
Lighting, dinnerware
c/o Baccarat, Inc.
11 East 26th St.
New York, NY 10010
(212) 696-1440

Haviland Limoges
Rue Philippe Lebon
87073 Limoges Cedex
France
33 (55) 04 73 00

HELLER DESIGNS, INC.
Dinnerware
41 Madison Ave.
New York, NY 10010
(212) 685-4200

HENREDON FURNITURE
INDUSTRIES, INC.
Upholstery
P.O. Box 70
Morganton, NC 28655
(704) 437-5261

HITACHI
Small appliances
Hitachi Home Electronics
(America) Inc.
401 W. Artesia Blvd.
Compton, CA 90220
(800) 241-6558
(213) 774-5151

Hitachi Sales Corporation
15-12 Nishi Shimbashi 2-Chome
Minato-ku
Tokyo 105
Japan

Hitachi Sales UK Ltd.
Hitachi House
Station Road
Hayes
Middlesex UB3 4DR
UK

H.U.D.D.L.E.®
Bath accessories
11159 Santa Monica Blvd.
Los Angeles, CA 90025
(310) 479-4769

HUTSCHENREUTHER
Dinnerware
Hutschenreuther Zentralvertrieb
Ludwigsmühle
8672 Selb
Germany
49 (9287) 730

Schott UK Retail Division
Drummond Rd.
Aston Fields Industrial Estate
Stafford ST16 3EL
UK
44 (785) 22 36 99

INTERIOR CRAFTS
Upholstery
614 Merchandise Mart
Chicago, IL 60654
(312) 943-3384

INTERLÜBKE
Storage
Interlübke Möbelfabrik
Postfach 1660
40-4840 Rheda-Weidenbrück
Germany

Interlübke Ltd.
239 Greenwich High Road
London SE10 8NB
UK
44 (81) 858 3325

JACQUES JUGEAT, INC.
Dinnerware
225 Fifth Ave., 10th Floor
New York, NY 10010
(212) 684-6760

See Robert Haviland & C. Parlon

JACUZZI® WHIRLPOOL™ BATH
Bath accessories
Subsid. of Hanson Industries
100 North Wiget La.
P.O. Drawer J
Walnut Creek, CA 94596
(510) 938-7070

KITCHENAID DIVISION
Small appliances
Whirlpool Customer Services
2303 Pipestone Rd.
Benton Harbor, MI 49022
(616) 927-7100

KNOLL INTERNATIONAL
Occasional
105 Wooster St.
New York, NY 10012
(212) 207-2200

Knoll International
20 Saville Row
London
W1X 1AE
UK

KOHLER CO.
Bath accessories
444 Highland Dr.
Kohler, WI 53044
(414) 457-4441

KOVACS, GEORGE
Lighting
See George Kovacs Lighting, Inc.

KROIN, INC.
Outdoor, bath accessories
180 Fawcett St.
Cambridge, MA 02138
(617) 492-4000

LANDES MANUFACTURING
CO., INC.
Outdoor
2824 East 11th St.
Los Angeles, CA 90023
(213) 264-8906

LIGHTOLIER, INC.
Lighting
100 Lighting Way
Secaucus, NJ 07096
(201) 864-3000

LIGNE ROSET
Upholstery
Ligne Roset
Div. of Gonin, Inc.
200 Lexington Ave.
New York, NY 10016
(212) 685-2238

Roset SA
BP 9
Briord
01470 Serrieres de Briord
France

Roset (UK) Ltd.
95a High Street
Great Missenden
Bucks
UK

LUXO LAMP CORP.
Lighting
36 Midland Ave.
Port Chester, NY 10573
(914) 937-4433

LYON-SHAW, INC.
Outdoor
Box 2069
1538 Jake Alexandria Blvd.
Salisbury, NC 28145
(704) 636-8720

McGUIRE CO.
Upholstery, occasional
1201 Bryant St.
San Francisco, CA 94103
(915) 986-0812

MEADOWCRAFT, INC.
Outdoor
P.O. Box 1357
Birmingham, AL 35201
(205) 853-2220

MELITTA
Kitchenware
Melitta, Inc.
1401 Berlin Rd.
Cherry Hill, NJ 08003
(609) 428-7202

MSS (UK) Ltd.
Clyde House
Reform Road
Maidenhead
Berkshire SL6 8BU
UK
44 (628) 777 888

Melitta Werke Bentz & Söhne
Ringstrasse 99
4950 Minden-Dützen
Germany

METRO KANE IMPORTS, LTD.
Small appliances
964 Third Ave.
9th Floor
New York, NY 10022
(212) 759-6262

MOULINEX
Small appliances
Moulinex Appliances Inc.
851 Seahawk Circle, Suite 105
Virginia Beach, VA 23452
(804) 468-4111

Moulinex Canada
10 Sims Crescent
Richmond Hill, Ontario
L4B 1K9
Canada

MUURAME
Storage
See Scandinavian Design, Inc.

NORELCO CONSUMER
PRODUCTS DIVISIONS
Small appliances, bath accessories
North American Philips Corp.
High Ridge Pk.
P.O. Box 10166
Stamford, CT 06904
(203) 329-2400

PFALTZGRAFF
Dinnerware
P.O. Box 1069
York, PA 17405
(717) 848-5500

POTTERY BARN, THE
Storage, dinnerware, kitchenware
231 Tenth Ave.
New York, NY 10011
(212) 206-8118

RANGINE CORP.
Storage
114 Union St.
Millis, MA 02054
(508) 376-4545

RICHARD GINORI CORP.
OF AMERICA
Dinnerware
41 Madison Ave.
New York, NY 10010

ROBERT HAVILAND &
C. PARLON
Dinnerware
Robert Haviland & C. Parlon
23 rue Hyacinthe-Faure
BP 1011
87050 Limoges
France

Lalique Ltd.
162 New Bond St.
London W14 9PA
UK
44 (71) 499 8228

See Jacques Jugeat, Inc.

ROBERT KRUPS
Small appliances, bath accessories
Robert Krups, N.A. Inc.
Reuten Drive
Closter, NJ 07624

Krups UK Ltd.
190 Camden St.
Birmingham B1 3DF
UK

Robert Krups GmbH & Co.
Heresbach Str. 29
5650 Solingen 19
Germany

ROBOT-COUPE
Small appliances
Robot-Coupe
Distibuted by European Home
Products
136 Washington St.
South Norwalk, CT 06854
(203) 866-9683

ICTC Ltd.
2 Fleming Way
Isleworth
Middlesex TW7 6EU
UK
44 (81) 847 2493

ROSENTHAL
Dinnerware
Rosenthal U.S.A., Ltd.
66-26 Metropolitan Ave.
Middle Village, NY 11379
(718) 417-3400

Rosenthal Glas und Porzellan AG
Postfach 1520
8672 Selb
Germany
49 (9287) 720

ROYAL COPENHAGEN
Dinnerware
Royal Copenhagen Porcelain
683 Madison Ave.
New York, NY 10021

Georg Jensen (Silversmiths)
Royal Copenhagen Porcelain Ltd.
15 New Bond Street
London W1Y 9PF
UK

Royal Copenhagen
6 Amagertorv
1160 Copenhagen K
Denmark
45 (33) 12 2686

ROYAL DOULTON
Dinnerware
Royal Doulton
Doulton & Co., Inc.
700 Cottontail La.
Somerset, NJ 08873
(908) 356-7880

Royal Doulton Tableware Ltd.
P.O. Box 301
Hobson Street
Burslem
Stoke-on-Trent
ST6 2AW
UK

ROYAL WORCESTER SPODE
Kitchenware
The Royal China Porcelain Co.
Subsid. of Royal Worcester Spode
1265 Glen Ave.
Moorestown, NJ 08057
(609) 866-2900

Royal Worcester Spode
Severn Street
Worcester WR1 2NE
UK
44 (905) 23221

RUBBERMAID, INC.
Storage, bath accessories
1147 Akron Rd.
Wooster, OH 44691
(216) 264-6464

SALTON/MAXIME
HOUSEWARES CORP.
Small appliances
550 Business Center Dr.
Kensington Center
Mt. Prospect, IL 60056
(800) 272-5629
(708) 803-4600

SAM FLAX, INC.
Occasional, storage
39 West 19th St.
New York, NY 10011
(212) 620-3000

SANYO
Small appliances
Sanyo/Fischer (USA) Corp.
21350 Lassen St.
Chatsworth, CA 91311
(818) 998-7322

Sanyo Electric Trading Co. Ltd.
33 Hiioshi-cho 2 Chome
Moriguchi-shi
Osaka
Japan

Sanyo UK
Sanyo House
Otterspool Way
Watford
Herts
WD2 8JX
UK

SCANDINAVIAN DESIGN, INC.
Storage
127 East 59th St.
New York, NY 10022
(212) 755-6078

SEARS, ROEBUCK & CO.
Small appliances
Sears Tower
Chicago, IL 60684
(312) 875-2500

SELIG MANUFACTURING
CO., INC.
Upholstery
P.O. Box 469
Siler City, NC 27344
(919) 742-4126

SHERLE WAGNER
INTERNATIONAL, INC.
Bath accessories
60 East 57th St.
New York, NY 10022
(212) 758-3300

STAR
Storage
Div. of Scanmark, Inc.
16641 Hale Ave.
Irvine, CA 92714
(714) 852-0656

SWAIM, INC.
Upholstery
1801 College Drive
High Point, NC 27260
(919) 885-6131

THAYER COGGIN, INC.
Upholstery, occasional, storage
230 South Rd.
P.O. Box 5867
High Point, NC 27262
(919) 841-6000

TREND PACIFIC
Dinnerware
See Pottery Barn

TRICONFORT
Outdoor
Triconfort, Inc.
200 Lexington Ave.
New York, NY 10016
(800) 833-9390

Triconfort
16 Avenue de Savoie
BP 703
38358 LaTour du Pin Cedex
St. Claire
France

VILETTA CHINA CO.
Dinnerware
8000 Harwin Dr. No. 150
Houston, TX 77036
(713) 785-0761

VILLEROY & BOCH
Dinnerware
Villeroy & Boch Tableware, Ltd.
41 Madison Ave.
New York, NY 10010

Villeroy and Boch Belgium SA
330 rue de Rollingergrund
Postfach 1808
L-1018
Luxembourg

WAGNER, SHERLE
Bath accessories
See Sherle Wagner International,
Inc.

WARING PRODUCTS
Small appliances
Div. of Dynamics Corp. of America
Rte. 44
New Hartford, CT 06057
(203) 379-0731

WATERCOLORS
Bath accessories
Watercolors, Inc.
Garrison-on-Hudson, NY 10524
(914) 424-3327

WATERFORD/WEDGWOOD USA
Dinnerware
Waterford/Wedgwood USA
41 Madison Ave.
New York, NY 10010
(212) 532-5950

Waterford/Wedgwood Ltd.
Barlaston
Stoke-on-Trent
Staffordshire ST12 9ES
UK
44 (7) 82 20 41 41

WATERWORKS
Bath accessories
1 Design Center Pl.
Suite 619
Boston, MA 02210
(617) 951-2496

WEIMAN CO.
Upholstery, occasional
Div. of Bassett Furniture
Industries, Inc.
Basset, VA 24055
(703) 629-7592

WEST BEND CO.
Small appliances
Div. of Premark International
P.O. Box 278
West Bend, WI 53095
(414) 334-2311

PHOTOGRAPHY CREDITS

Jacket: © Keith Scott Morton. Pages 2–3: © Jacques Dirand. Page 6: © Eleni Mylonas/Jackson. Page 8: © David Vestal/ Jackson.

ROMANTIC WHITES. Pages 12, 14–15, 18–23, 25, 32–33, 36–37, 39, 40–41: © Keith Scott Morton. Pages 24, 34: Frank Kolleogy, © 1980 and © 1981 *Mademoiselle*, courtesy Condé Nast Publications. Pages 26–29: © Jacques Dirand. Pages 30–31: © Paul Warchol, ESTO. Page 35, left: © Joe Standart, courtesy West Point Pepperell; right, top: Deborah Turbeville, © 1982 *Mademoiselle*, courtesy Condé Nast Publications; right, center: © Antoine Rozés with stylist Claire Hirsch-Marie, La Maison de Marie Claire; right, bottom: © James Levin, courtesy Dan River. Page 38: © Krysztof Pruszkowski.

RUSTIC WHITES. Page 42: © Lilo Raymond/Jackson. Pages 44–45: © Eleni Mylonas/Jackson. Pages 48–49, 58–61, 62, 64–69: © Keith Scott Morton. Pages 50–51: © André Gillardin. Page 52: Feliciano, © 1979 *House & Garden*, courtesy Condé Nast Publications. Page 53: courtesy Doug Atwill. Pages 54–55: © Bent Rej. Page 56: courtesy David Howard. Page 57, top: © Jean-Claude Nicolas with stylist Marie-Paul Pellé, La Maison de Marie Claire; center: Ernst Beadle © 1979 *House & Garden*, courtesy Condé Nast Publications; bottom: Russell Macmasters. Page 63, top: David Massey, © 1980 *House & Garden*, courtesy Condé Nast Publications; bottom: © Joe Standart, courtesy Martex/West Point Pepperell.

REFINED WHITES. Pages 70, 76–77, 84–85, 94, 95 top, 96–103: © Keith Scott Morton. Pages 72–73: © Raeanne Giovanni. Pages 78–79: © Charles Nesbit. Pages 80–81: Gene Maggio, *The New York Times*. Pages 82–83: © Tom Yee. Pages 86–89: © Kari Haavisti, courtesy Marimekko. Pages 90–91: © Carla de Benedetti. Pages 92–93: courtesy David Hicks France. Page 95, bottom: Lynn Karlin, © 1980 *Mademoiselle*, courtesy Condé Nast Publications. Pages 104–105: © Charles Nesbit, courtesy Alan Buchsbaum.

RATIONAL WHITES. Pages 106, 118–119: © Richard Payne, courtesy Charles Gwathmey. Pages 108–109: © Norman McGrath, courtesy Charles Gwathmey. Pages 112–115: Ezra Stoller, © ESTO. Pages 116–117: © Marlene Schneider–Schnelle. Page 120, top left: courtesy Poggenpohl; bottom left: Frank Kolleogy, © 1979 *Mademoiselle*, courtesy Condé Nast Publications; top right: courtesy Mariette Himes Gomez; bottom right: courtesy Formica Corp. Page 121: © Hedrich-Blessing, courtesy Marvin Ullman AIA. Pages 122–123: © Raeanne Giovanni. Page 124, top: © Tom Yee; center: courtesy Alfredo de Vido; bottom: © Norman McGrath, courtesy William Ellis AIA. Page 125: © Peter Aaron, ESTO. Pages 126–127: © Robert Lautman, courtesy Hugh Newell Jacobsen FAIA. Pages 128–131: © Balthazar Korab.

RAREFIED WHITES. Page 132: © Jean-Luis Siepp with stylist Anne-Marie Comte, La Maison de Marie Claire. Pages 134–135, 140–141, 144–145, 148, 152–153, 155, 162–163: © Keith Scott Morton. Pages 138–139, 142, bottom: © Oberto Gili. Page 142, top: © Norman McGrath. Page 143: © Ken Druse. Pages 146–147: © Wolfgang Hoyt, ESTO. Page 149, top: courtesy Diane Carulli; bottom: © Peter Aaron, ESTO. Pages 150–151: © Uwe Ommer with stylist Claire Hirsch-Marie, La Maison de Marie Claire. Page 154: courtesy Elizabeth McClintock. Pages 156–157: © Peter Bosch. Pages 158–159: © Carla de Benedetti. Pages 160–161: © Gösta Peterson. Pages 164–167: © Lynn Karlin.

RESORT WHITES. Page 168: courtesy Las Hadas Hotel and Resort. Pages 170–171: © Bo Niles. Pages 174–175: © Jacques Dirand with stylist Claire Hirsch-Marie, La Maison de Marie Claire. Pages 176–177: © Transworld Feature Syndicate. Pages 178–179: © Charles White, courtesy Waldo's Designs. Pages 180–181: © Raymond Waites, courtesy GEAR Inc. Pages 182–183: © James Mortimer, The World of Interiors. Pages 184–185: © Michael Dunne, courtesy Barbara Littman. Pages 186–187: © Balthazar Korab. Pages 188–189: © Bent Rej. Pages 190–191: © Keith Scott Morton.

ACKNOWLEDGMENTS

Many people participated in the intimate process of bringing *White by Design* into being and I thank them all for their gifts of time, laughter and encouragement.

Long ago, as a young girl, I spent a summer in a house overlooking the Mediterranean Sea. Drawn into the wake of my parents' dearest dream—to pause and concentrate totally on painting and music—my sisters and I entered into that sojourn as into a fairy tale. That summer was a pause, an intermission, and it changed the tenor and direction of our lives. Soon after, we returned to Italy to live, and it was then that my parents made a lifelong commitment to their art.

Whiteness—the sun-impregnated light and space we encountered in Italy—seemed to enwrap us, seemed to create a feeling of expectancy somewhere between inspiration and invention. I recall my mother's white studio with her still, white canvases resting on their easels anticipating color; and I remember my father's white workroom with his piano and his still, white pages awaiting orchestrations. Their white rooms inspired them, and they inspired my sisters and me. I thank my parents, Ann and Francis Thorne, for that sojourn; in a special way they and my sisters, Wendy and Candy, have lived inside this book from the very beginning.

Bill, my husband, and David and Peter, my sons, honored my solitude and I embrace them for their acceptance of the time it took for me to complete this work.

Jonathan Dolger, a literary agent and my neighbor, and Susan Meyer and Marsha Melnick of Roundtable Press, encouraged me to transform the early idea for the book into a concrete proposal. Rachel Newman, my editor during my nine-year tenure at *Country Living* magazine, granted time to shoot specific locations and also gave me a month's leave of absence during which I was able to read and write without interruption. Keith Morton photographed these locations; without his understanding and humor these rooms would not have appeared as honest and clear as they do. To all, I extend my gratitude.

The other photographers, and the designers, architects, and homeowners, who are represented here of course make up the content of the book. It is a very special pleasure to include them; I have admired all of them over the years and am honored that they joined in this effort.

Ralph Lauren offers a foreword that is direct and to the point. I am indebted to him for lending his personal thoughts about white to this book.

Julio Vega, the designer of *White by Design*, brought the very qualities—space and light—that I appreciate most in architecture and interiors into these pages and, in so doing, transformed the book into a work of art.